THE
HISTORY
CHANNEL®
PRESENTS

HAUNTED HISTORY™

GHOSTLY GRAVEYARDS AND SPOOKY SPOTS

Read all the books in

THE
HISTORY
CHANNEL®
PRESENTS

HAUNTED HISTORY™

GHOSTLY GRAVEYARDS AND SPOOKY SPOTS

By Cameron Banks

SCHOLASTIC INC.

New York   Toronto   London   Auckland   Sydney
Mexico City   New Delhi   Hong Kong   Buenos Aires

No part of this work may be reproduced in whole or in
part, stored in a retrieval system, or transmitted in any
form or by any means, electronic, mechanical, photocopy-
ing, recording, or otherwise, without written permission of
the publisher. For information regarding permission, write
to Scholastic Inc., Attention: Permissions Department,
557 Broadway, New York, NY 10012.

ISBN 0-439-55705-4

The History Channel, the 'H' logo, and HAUNTED
HISTORY are trademarks of A&E Television Networks. ©
2003 A&E Television Networks.
All rights reserved. Published by Scholastic Inc.
SCHOLASTIC and associated logos are trademarks and/or
registered trademarks of Scholastic Inc.

Designed by Louise Bova

12 11 10 9 8 7 6   4 5 6 7 8/0

Printed in the U.S.A.
First printing, September 2003

Visit Scholastic.com for information about our
books and authors online!

CONTENTS

DO YOU DARE GO THERE?

It would definitely be cool to visit Philadelphia, Savannah, Washington, D.C., Chicago, and San Francisco because the histories of those cities are so interesting. But stopping at historic places is about to get a whole lot cooler – *bone-chilling*, in fact!

Many people believe that these cities are home to spooks of all sorts! From Civil War specters in Savannah, Georgia, to the ghosts of gangsters in Chicago, Illinois, interesting varieties of spirits populate these historic cities. And from phantom patriots in Philadelphia, Pennsylvania, and Washington, D.C., to strange spirits in San Francisco, California, the supernatural is often said to be part of the scenery!

Working with The History Channel®, we've ventured to some of the scariest sites in American history. We've tracked down stories of amazing apparitions, such as ghosts of the famous and poltergeists who pelt people with objects! We've found real-life people who swear they've witnessed hauntings — including a queen and a couple of U.S. presidents. And, of course, we want to share those stories with you!

So join us as we explore America's ghostly graveyards and spooky spots... if you *dare*!

SAN FRANCISCO

CHICAGO

GRAVEYARD

PHILADELPHIA, PENNSYLVANIA

FOUNDING PHANTOMS (AND OTHER SPIRITS OF INDEPENDENCE)

Home to Independence Hall and the Liberty Bell, Philadelphia, Pennsylvania, is full of historic sites and true American spirit. It's where some of our country's most famous figures lived ... and died. Not surprisingly, Philadelphia is also home to spirit sightings that are practically a "Who's Who" of America's haunted history!

Birthplace of Liberty

Philadelphia was the first settlement in the colony of Pennsylvania, which William Penn founded in 1682. The city was the birthplace of the American Revolution, where great statesmen such as George Washington, Thomas Jefferson, and Benjamin Franklin once walked the streets. By the mid-1700s, Philadelphia was the largest city in the American colonies.

On July 4, 1776, members from each of the thirteen colonies gathered in the Pennsylvania Statehouse — now known as Independence Hall — to sign a document called the Declaration of Independence. Many say that the ghosts of our nation's Founding Fathers are *still* hanging around Independence Hall. . . .

Independent Spirits

For years, strange phenomena have occurred in Independence Hall! Everyone from tourists to National Park Service rangers have reported seeing wispy figures, hearing weird noises, and feeling icy chills as they walked through the building.

In 1994, one National Park Service ranger reported an encounter that goes *beyond* strange. The ranger was closing up the building and setting alarms for the night. Out of the corner of his eye, he saw someone standing at the foot of the staircase. The fig-

THE PHANTOM FILES

The name Philadelphia comes from two ancient Greek words: *philo–*, which means "love," and *adelphos*, meaning "brother." Together, the words make *Philadelphia*, which means "City of Brotherly Love."

ure was dressed in the clothing of Colonial times!

According to the park ranger, the figure took two or three steps up the staircase . . . then vanished! The ranger did his duty and finished closing up. But, needless to say, he got out of there *fast*!

Dancing Ben

Benjamin Franklin was an extraordinary writer, publisher, and inventor, and he helped draft the Declaration of Independence. In later years, his influence and intelligence helped our country establish the Senate and Congress and adopt the Constitution. This remarkable man spent much of his life in Philadelphia.

And he may be there still,

PARANORMAL POP QUIZ!

In a private mansion in Philadelphia, a two-hundred-year-old wingback chair is nicknamed "the Death Chair," because people who sit in it tend to die shortly afterward! True or false?

(Answer: *True* — and superscary, too!)

Benjamin Franklin

5

long after his death. Eyewitnesses have seen Franklin's restless spirit at various locations throughout the city. His favorite spot, some say, is the Library Hall of the American Philosophical Society, which he helped found in 1743.

Many claim that Franklin's energetic spirit even lives on in the streets of Philadelphia, coming to life out of an old statue. Legend has it that the wise old statesman is sometimes seen *dancing* through the City of Brotherly Love!

THE PHANTOM FILES

One of Philadelphia's most renowned residents in the 1800s was famous writer Edgar Allan Poe. Poe is best known for his creepy poems and terrifying tales, such as "The Raven" and "The Pit and the Pendulum." Since his death in 1849, the ghost of Poe is said to haunt locations all over the city.

STARS AND STRIPES . . . FOREVER?

The Betsy Ross House on Philadelphia's Arch Street was the home of the celebrated woman who sewed America's first flag. Her house is one of the most popular historic tourist sites in Philadelphia, with more than 300,000 visitors a year. And it may also be haunted by the patriotic woman who resided there!

A New Flag

At the start of the American Revolution, Colonial patriots had to create a unified fighting force. And to bring the colonies together, they needed a national symbol of unity — a flag.

In 1776, patriots turned to Betsy Ross, a widow who ran a Philadelphia upholstery shop. Would she help design and sew the first flag of the new nation? The answer, fortunately, was yes. Ross's original design — white stars in a blue box and red-and-white stripes — still lives on today as the symbol of America. And many say that Ross's spirit is also still around today!

A Polite Phantom

Visitors to the Betsy Ross House claim to have spotted her ghost in the room that was her old bedroom. In fact, some say she is seen standing at the foot of her old bed!

What's even stranger, many report *hearing* the

PARANORMAL POP QUIZ!

Author Bram Stoker wrote a major part of his horror classic, *Dracula*, while staying in Philadelphia. True or false?

(Answer: *True*)

patriotic old seam-stress in the house! In the basement, they say they've heard the sound of someone whispering, "Pardon me, pardon me" again and again. When the witnesses looked around, nobody was there!

Could it be the ghost of Betsy Ross herself, rushing past to quickly finish the flag? No one knows for sure. But it's clear that whomever — or *whatever* — is in the base-ment of the Betsy Ross House has good manners!

THE PHANTOM FILES

For years, unexplained bloodcurdling screams have been heard at Fort Mifflin. Just how bad are these screams? On at least one occasion, people have called the police to investigate the terrible sound, believing a woman was being attacked there! When the police arrived, nobody was found. . . .

PHANTOMS AT FORT MIFFLIN

American patriots built Philadelphia's Fort Mifflin during the Revolutionary War. Today, the fort's four-teen buildings and fifty acres are now open to the public as a National Historic Landmark — and are said to be home to numerous spirits!

Brave Battling

In 1777, the American patriots' Continental Navy flag flew proudly over Fort Mifflin. When the British attacked the fort, the colonists fought valiantly, destroying a major battleship. But after five days of murderous assaults by the British, American Major Simeon Thayer gave orders to the patriots to abandon the fort.

But Major Thayer left the flag flying, which sent a clear message to the British: "We don't surrender!" A replica of the flag still flies over the fort in honor of the 250 patriots who gave their lives there. And according to legend, the legacy of the Fort Mifflin men who fought for freedom lives on . . . because the site is said to be swirling with ghosts!

PARANORMAL POP QUIZ!

Spirits can sometimes take the form of ectoplasm — a pale, foglike substance that resembles streaks of light and mist. True or false?

(Answer: True)

9

THE PHANTOM FILES

At one time, Fort Mifflin held four hundred prisoners in dark, dungeonlike bunkers. It's said that the ghosts of prisoners of war are still there — including a soldier who nods to visitors . . . but has *no face!*

Colonial Specters

Fort Mifflin visitors claim that a person in a Colonial uniform sits near the artillery shed, cleaning a gun. They think the man is an employee in costume. That would make sense except for one thing: No employees wear costumes at Fort Mifflin!

Visitors may be seeing a soldier spirit known as "Amos" who is often spotted at the site. Sometimes he looks up at them, and sometimes he doesn't, witnesses say. It's not clear whether he sees the visitors . . . but they claim to see *him*!

The ghostly figure known as the "Lamplighter" is another Fort Mifflin resident that many visitors have witnessed. The specter is seen walking slowly and carefully, making his way past the Soldiers' Barracks. The figure appears only at dusk, perhaps to light the way for other long-departed spirits. . . .

EASTERN STATE PENITENTIARY

When Philadelphia's Eastern State Penitentiary

opened in 1829, it was the most expensive building in the United States — and soon became one of the most famous! Now a museum, the former prison resembles a huge, Gothic-style castle. And it's said that the ghosts of some criminals from the past may linger there.

Eerie Sights and Sounds

Even those who don't believe in ghosts have felt the eerie pull of Eastern State Penitentiary. Sean Kelley, the site's program director, says, "It can be unnerving,

PARANORMAL POP QUIZ!

One of Eastern State Penitentiary's best-known spirits is a poltergeist who talks — and talks and talks and talks — and who is said to have driven several inmates insane over the years. True or false?

(Answer: False. There are other ghosts who are said to dwell here, but not this one!)

even to a big skeptic like me." Not long ago, at the administration building, Kelley was getting ready to do some work when he heard strange sounds. "I could have sworn [that] on the floor above us I could hear people murmuring, and footsteps. . . . It was creepy," says Kelley.

Some say that, in the cell blocks, there is a strange feeling of tension and pressure. Although there are no records of executions at the prison, hundreds — or even thousands — of people died there. It's said that those eternal prisoners may still haunt the jail with old anguish and pain.

And if weird sounds and sensations don't convince visitors the prison is haunted, seeing spirits certainly does! Tourists have reported seeing fleeting figures that dart from cell to cell — when no other living people were on the cell block!

THE PHANTOM FILES

Edgar Allan Poe first visited the General Wayne Inn in 1839 and is said to have written a major part of his poem "The Raven" while staying there in 1843. Over the years, his spirit has been seen sitting at his favorite corner table!

GHOSTS AT THE GENERAL WAYNE INN

Opened in 1704 and considered to be the longest-running restaurant in the United States, the General Wayne once welcomed famous historic figures such as Benjamin Franklin, George Washington, the Marquis de Lafayette, and Edgar Allan Poe, along with soldiers and other travelers. The inn is also considered to be one of the most haunted locations in the country!

Skulking Soldiers?

The General Wayne Inn is said to have been home to a great number of ghosts — seventeen, to be exact! Several of these spirits are military men, including the ghost of a tall soldier that was first witnessed in 1848.

THE PHANTOM FILES

From 1790 until 1800, Philadelphia was the nation's capital. It even called itself the Athens of America because of its rich cultural, political, and intellectual life.

Local lore claims that the soldier was murdered, and his body was buried in the inn's stone walls almost three hundred years ago. Over the years, the soldier has reportedly been seen lurking in the shadows near the wine cellar.

In fact, according to Carol Scott, the inn's manager, a worker recently encountered the apparition in the basement. "He swears that he saw something that looked as if [it was wearing] white leggings and a blue jacket dash across this one area of the basement," Ms. Scott says. "It freaked him out!"

Creepy Close Encounters

Some spirits at the General Wayne Inn like to get up close and personal! Late one evening, two workers were alone in the building. As one man wiped down the counter, he heard a squeak on the wooden floor . . . then felt a tap on his shoulder!

He looked around and found no one there. Soon the worker heard another strange sound. Someone was whistling somewhere in the restaurant . . . but there wasn't a soul in sight! To this day, there is still no way to explain what he *heard* — or why.

THE PHANTOM FILES

At the General Wayne Inn, employees often report hearing a single scream in the middle of the night. According to manager Carol Scott, the scream sounds like it is coming from a man. Who — or what — produces the unearthly sound? That, like so many other haunted happenings, still remains a mystery!

The same might be said of *all* of Philadelphia's ghostly sightings. Do the spirits of our Founding Fathers, long-ago soldiers — and others — still linger in Philadelphia? Some say yes, while others are more skeptical. But one thing is sure: Philadelphia is a fascinating place to visit . . . whether or not you believe in ghosts!

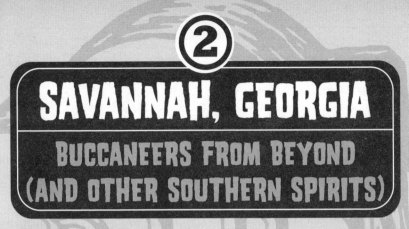

② SAVANNAH, GEORGIA

BUCCANEERS FROM BEYOND (AND OTHER SOUTHERN SPIRITS)

With its elegant old mansions and lush parks, Savannah has been called "the most beautiful city in North America." It's also been called one of the most haunted! If you're one of the seven million tourists who visit Savannah each year, you just might meet the spirit of a seafarer, soldier, or one of the many other restless ghosts said to reside in the city.

THE PIRATES' HOUSE

Savannah's Pirates' House was originally built in 1754 as a seaman's inn and is a famous restaurant today. Back in the mid-1700s, it was also a hangout for sailors — not to mention smugglers, criminals, and pirates from around the world! Many say these rough characters still pay visits to the house. . . .

Real-Life *Treasure Island*?

In *Treasure Island*, the famous pirate novel by

Robert Louis Stevenson, the character Captain Flint gives a map of the island to Billy Bones while on his deathbed. Legend says that the scene was based on a real-life encounter that took place at the Pirates' House. In fact, many people believe that Stevenson based the character of Captain Flint on a real person — whose ghost now wanders the restaurant!

One evening, the manager of the restaurant closed the Pirates' House for the night and came to see Herb Traub, a former owner of the restaurant. "He was visibly excited and visibly quite shook up," says Traub of the manager. The manager swore he'd suddenly seen a man sitting in a chair at a table — but when he turned around to get a better look, the man had vanished!

Was it the ghost of a long-gone buccaneer? Nobody knows for sure. But the manager was certain he'd seen something — perhaps something supernatural! "He was genuinely scared. . . . He was shaking," recalls Traub.

Secret Tunnels

There is evidence that a secret tunnel once ran from the old inn's rum cellar to the Savannah waterfront. Some Savannians say that pirates would kidnap young men visiting the inn and take them through the tunnel to waiting ships. This is how many pirate ships got their crew members!

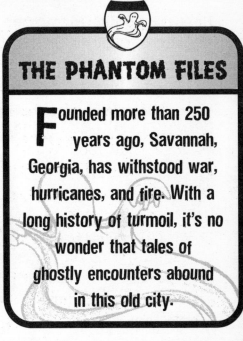

THE PHANTOM FILES

Founded more than 250 years ago, Savannah, Georgia, has withstood war, hurricanes, and fire. With a long history of turmoil, it's no wonder that tales of ghostly encounters abound in this old city.

Several decades ago, when the tunnel was still open, it is said that a Savannah man decided to explore it. As he slowly made his way through the dark, dank passageway, his foot struck an object in the dirt. Gathering up his courage, he pressed on.

Finally, he came to a dead end — a solid wall. But he felt he was no longer *alone* in the deserted tunnel. Suddenly, he heard the sound of approaching footsteps and voices. The man pressed himself against a damp wall as a group of shadowy figures marched by in a blast of icy air. Chilled to the bone and speechless, the man couldn't believe what he saw next. The group of figures kept right on walking, passing through the solid wall as if it didn't exist!

Needless to say, the terrified explorer beat a hasty retreat! He vowed never to enter the tunnel again.

BONAVENTURE CEMETERY

Oak trees laden with Spanish moss and magnificent monuments make Bonaventure Cemetery one of the loveliest locations in Savannah. It is so beautiful, say some Savannians, that being dead and buried at Bonaventure is almost as good as being alive anywhere else!

The final resting place of statesmen, war heroes, and celebrities, Bonaventure is the site of Savannah's oldest ghost story. And many say that, for years, it has been a very special place for spirit sightings.

THE PHANTOM FILES

Savannah's prosperity in the early 1800s came with a terrible price: the forced labor of slaves. Legalized in Georgia in 1750, slavery brought thousands of people from Africa and the West Indies to work on the city's docks and nearby plantations. It's said that you can still hear the dreadful moans of the people who were kept in chains and sold into slavery at the Savannah waterfront.

A Never-ending Toast?

More than two hundred years ago, Bonaventure was one of the most magnificent plantations in the South. It was originally owned by Colonel Josiah Tattnall, a Revolutionary War hero and former governor of Georgia. The Tattnall home at Bonaventure was considered Savannah's most impressive manor — until it was destroyed one fateful day in 1800.

It was Christmastime, and the colonel was giving a grand holiday party in the dining room. Suddenly, the house caught on fire! Fortunately, nobody was hurt. But legend has it that the colonel simply ordered the table to be taken to the plantation lawn, where guests finished

PARANORMAL POP QUIZ!

Ghosts are sighted only at places where they experienced pain, loss, or unhappiness, say experts. True or false?

(Answer: False. Sometimes ghosts appear in places where they once had fun!)

their meal! The guests and the colonel began to exchange toasts, and they cried, "May the joy of this occasion never end!" According to the story, the meal ended with Colonel Tattnall throwing his crystal goblet at an oak tree, and all the guests followed his lead. In the meantime, the fire in the house raged on. The manor at Bonaventure was never rebuilt, and eventually, the plantation's gardens and terraces became a cemetery. But, some say, that long-ago night's festivities live forever. . . .

THE PHANTOM FILES

The ghost of patriot James Habersham Jr. may still watch over the Olde Pink House restaurant, the only surviving eighteenth-century mansion in Savannah. Many say the spirit of Habersham, a member of the Liberty Boys who plotted against the British in the 1770s, appears in Colonial dress in the restaurant. The heroic ghost allegedly likes to light candles and rearrange furniture!

Party On!

Witnesses swear that the happy spirit of Josiah Tattnall still entertains his guests on the beautiful old grounds of Bonaventure. If you are passing by the cemetery on certain nights, they say that you can hear the festive crash of crystal wine-glasses and the sounds of laughter.

Some people claim they have even seen the phantoms who party at Bonaventure! Ghostly guests, wearing old-fashioned fancy dress, appear on the old plantation grounds at night, some say. (Talk about the party *never* ending!)

PARANORMAL POP QUIZ!

Ghost sightings are often preceded by an eerie feeling that someone else is in the room — even if it appears that nobody is there.

True or false?

(Answer: *True*)

CIVIL WAR SPIRITS

In 1861, the Civil War began when a group of Southern states, called the Confederacy, decided to leave — or secede from — the Union, or Northern states. Savannah Confederates seized control of Fort Jackson, a stronghold that dates back to the Revolutionary War. Troops eventually evacuated the fort when General Sherman's Union army marched there in 1864, but some of its soldiers may still fight on today.

Fort Jackson Specters

Many visitors and guides at Fort Jackson have witnessed ghostly apparitions dressed in Confederate gray uniforms. According to James Mack Adams, a local author, one of the fort's employees met a ghost dressed in a Civil War cap and jacket — on her first day at work! "She said the figure stood there for just a few seconds, then he turned and walked out. Well, this affected the young lady so much that the next day, she called to say she was quitting and she never came back," he reports.

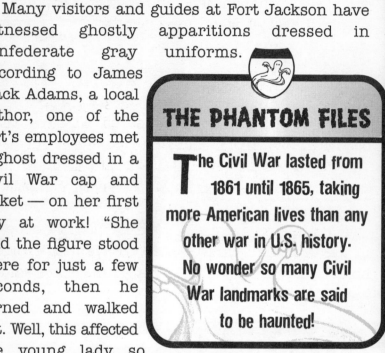

THE PHANTOM FILES

The Civil War lasted from 1861 until 1865, taking more American lives than any other war in U.S. history. No wonder so many Civil War landmarks are said to be haunted!

One of the ghostly soldiers at Fort Jackson is said to be the spirit of one Private Garrity, who, long ago, attacked and killed an officer at the fort. He threw himself into the moat surrounding the fort, and before anyone could save him, he drowned.

No one knows why Garrity attacked the officer. But over the years, visitors have claimed to have encountered a Confederate soldier as they cross the moat. Perhaps it is Private Garrity, condemned to guard Fort Jackson for *eternity*!

Marshall House

When Union General William Tecumseh Sherman marched through Georgia in 1864, the people of Savannah surrendered to save their beautiful city from being burned to the ground. Ten thousand battered Confederate soldiers fled, and Sherman took control of Savannah in late December.

General Sherman set up a makeshift hospital in the Marshall House, one of Savannah's oldest hotels. The Union soldiers treated there are said to haunt the place to this day!

Living Bones?

During the Civil War, the conditions in military hospitals challenged even the most skillful doctors. Overcrowding, rampant disease, and little or no anesthesia for operations resulted in terrible suffering and many deaths. With little space to dispose of amputated limbs or dead bodies, many body parts ended up in the Marshall House basement. During a renovation in the 1990s, workers found a number of *human bones*!

Ghosts who may "belong" to those bones are said to haunt the hotel today. Since the Marshall House reopened, several guests have reported seeing an apparition who wears the blue uniform of a Union soldier. Was the sighting for real? To find out, the hotel called in some experts.

"The Searchers"

In the summer of 1999, a group of paranormal investigators, known as "the Searchers," came to the Marshall House to see what, if any, ghostly activity was present there. According to investigator Beth Ronberg, members of the group believed that a Union soldier was indeed still at the hotel, wandering the basement halls!

And there may be other strange spirits staying at the hotel. Some say they have encountered a ghostly little girl who likes to

PARANORMAL POP QUIZ!

An exorcism is a ritual that spiritual leaders perform to get rid of evil spirits. True or false?

(Answer: *True*)

tickle guests' feet! There have also been claims of strange, unexplained noises. It seems the Marshall

House has its fair share of specters. But why?

The answer may lie in past history and personal tragedy. According to Beth Ronberg, spooked sites like the Marshall House hold spirits that are still confused about their place in the world, long after death. "If a person has a very tragic death, a lot of times they don't go where they're supposed to go," says Ronberg. "They wind up being stuck in a place. . . . They don't understand that they are supposed to move on."

THE PHANTOM FILES

Jim Williams, the subject of the best-selling book *Midnight in the Garden of Good and Evil,* was so disturbed by mysterious footsteps, cold spots, and unearthly screams in his Savannah mansion that he had an Episcopal bishop perform an exorcism in the house — and later moved out!

THE JULIETTE GORDON LOW HOUSE

Not all hauntings, however, involve horrible tragedy. One of Savannah's most famous ghost sightings surrounds a tale of eternal love. It's said that "till death do us part" takes on new meaning in one of Savannah's magnificent mansions.

Juliette Gordon Low was the founder of the Girl Scouts of America. She grew up in a Regency-style house built in 1818 with many brothers and sisters and her parents, William and Nellie Gordon.

When General Gordon died in 1912, his wife, Nellie, was heartbroken. In her remaining years, she spoke constantly of the day when she would join her beloved husband. And, say witnesses, Nellie *did* reunite five years later with her cherished husband — in spirit form!

PARANORMAL POP QUIZ!

According to paranormal investigators, spirits almost always seem somber or in distress. True or false?

(Answer: False. Some ghosts are reported to be cheerful and are even heard laughing!)

A Caller from Beyond

In 1917, Nellie lay close to death in the house she had shared with the general — and something very strange occurred. Nellie's grandson Arthur Gordon recalls, "My grandfather, who had been dead five or six years, came through the door and passed through the room. . . ."

The apparition said nothing and simply kept moving along. Even Morrison, the family's elderly butler, was shocked to see General Gordon come walking down the front stairs! As Arthur Gordon reports, "Morrison said all he knew was that the general had come down the stairs, passed by him without speaking, and gone out the front door. Morrison thought that perhaps he'd come to bring his wife back with him."

Did the two people imagine seeing General Gordon at the same time? Or was it a real haunting? We'll never know for sure, but since that day in 1917, many have reported phantom footsteps at the Juliette Gordon Low House. Perhaps the ghost of General Gordon continues to visit. (Or is it

THE PHANTOM FILES

At the Hamilton-Turner House (a bed-and-breakfast), the house's happy former occupants may still be in residence! It's said that the long-gone Hamilton children, who once lived on the top floor of the mansion, sometimes keep guests awake at night rolling balls across the floor and giggling together!

just someone delivering Girl Scout cookies?)

In stately old Savannah, you're never far from the city's remarkable past — and possibly, from the strange spirits said to roam there. So next time you hop on a riverboat, set foot in a historic home, or take a late-night stroll through a Savannah cemetery, remember to keep your eyes peeled for the strange and unexplained. You never know what you might find!

In 1891, the *Washington Star* newspaper called Washington, D.C., "America's greatest haunted city." More than a hundred years later, many say that the Federal City is still one of the spookiest places around. In fact, some swear that heroes from American history may still hang out in Washington!

PARANORMAL POP QUIZ!

Dolley Madison lived her entire adult life at the White House. True or false?

(Answer: False. After her husband's death, Dolley Madison lived on Lafayette Square near the White House — where her spirit has also been spotted!)

WHITE HOUSE HAUNTINGS

Built as a home for America's presidents in the 1790s, the White House — also known as the

Executive Mansion — has a long and colorful history of hauntings. Over the years, servants and heads of state alike say they have encountered the supernatural in America's most famous residence!

Phantom First Lady

Dolley Madison, wife of the fifth U.S. president, James Madison, was known for her lavish entertaining style and the elaborate rose garden she created on the White House grounds some 200 years ago. In fact, some say that Dolley loved her garden so much that she'll never leave it!

In the early 1900s, President

PARANORMAL POP QUIZ!

The White House was not built in time for first President George Washington and his family to move in, so the building's first occupants were the family of President John Adams, America's second president.
True or false?

(Answer: True)

Woodrow Wilson's wife decided to have White House gardeners move the roses that Mrs. Madison had lovingly planted centuries earlier. Minutes after the gardeners began working, it's said that the figure of Dolley Madison appeared, screaming and waving her arms. Spooked, the gardeners dropped their tools and ran. The White House Rose Garden remains today — a beautiful legacy of Dolley Madison!

THE PHANTOM FILES

When President John Adams and his wife, Abigail, moved into the White House, the First Lady used the mansion's East Room for drying her family's clothes. It must have been a great laundry room, because some say Abigail Adams is still seen there, carrying a basket of wet clothes!

Midnight Encounter with Abraham Lincoln

By far, the most amazing reports of supernatural encounters in Washington, D.C., involve the apparition of America's sixteenth president, Abraham Lincoln. "Honest Abe" is said to have revealed himself to a royal visitor at the White House — and even to another president!

Queen Wilhelmina of the Netherlands stayed at

the White House in the 1940s. One night, shortly after midnight, she claimed she heard a knock at her door, opened it, and saw Abraham Lincoln standing in the doorway. At the time, Lincoln had been dead for more than eighty years! The Queen fainted on the spot.

Knock, Knock ... It's the President!

President Harry S. Truman did not possess a strong belief in the supernatural. But, in his diary, he also recorded meeting President Lincoln at the White House!

THE PHANTOM FILES

Abraham Lincoln believed that dreams were part reality. Shortly before he was assassinated by John Wilkes Booth in 1865, Lincoln confided to a colleague that he had dreamed of his own death! In the dream, he heard sobbing coming from the White House's East Room. He walked into the room and asked a mourner who had died. She said, "The assassinated president." When Lincoln looked inside the coffin, he saw himself!

Late one evening, Truman, like Queen Wilhelmina, answered a knock at his door. Peering out into the hallway, the President saw that no one was there ... but he felt something. A bone-chilling

Abraham Lincoln

sensation of cold enveloped him as he heard footsteps trailing down the hallway.

For no known reason, President Truman was convinced that the visitor was none other than Abraham Lincoln, who had resided in the White House nearly a century earlier!

Modern-day Mysteries

To this day, tales of supernatural encounters at the White House persist. It's said that, at night, a long-dead usher is still turning off lights in the Executive Mansion and that the ghost of a White House doorman occasionally appears, ready to work!

Recent White House residents have also reported feeling the presence of something strange and unexplained. In a 1996 interview with Rosie O'Donnell, former First Lady Hillary Clinton said, "There is something about the [White] House at night that makes you just feel like you are summoning up the spirits of all the people who have lived there, and worked there, and walked through the halls there."

The former First Lady added, "It's neat. It can be a little creepy."

FRIENDLY NEIGHBORHOOD GHOSTS

The White House may be a center of Washington's ghostly folklore — but experiences with spirits in the city don't end at the Executive Mansion's gates! The neighborhood immediately surrounding the presidential residence is *teeming* with the ghosts of politics past.

THE PHANTOM FILES

Great Britain's Prime Minister Winston Churchill is said to have refused to sleep in the Lincoln Bedroom at the White House after he, too, spotted President Abraham Lincoln's ghost lurking there!

The Specters of the Willard Hotel

The Willard Hotel was built in 1816 and soon became one of the most important meeting places in Washington, D.C. A home away from home for kings, diplomats, and celebrities for nearly two centuries, the Willard may still host long-gone guests from the past.

While the Willard has long been the most prominent residence for dignitaries visiting the capital, one of the hotel's most devoted guests actually lived just blocks away! After a hard day in the Oval Office, President Ulysses S. Grant would stroll over to the Willard's lobby, sit in his favorite chair, and smoke a cigar.

The Willard (now called the Willard Intercontinental) is still known as the "residence of presidents" . . . and many modern-day visitors claim to have felt the presence of Ulysses S. Grant in the hotel's lobby! President Grant's spirit is said to make itself known through the distinctive aroma of his fine cigars. Occasionally, visitors are said to smell their scent in the lobby — when nobody's smoking!

THE PHANTOM FILES

During his presidency from 1869 to 1877, Ulysses S. Grant visited the Willard's lobby nearly every afternoon. As his fondness for the Willard's lobby became well known more people began to come in to the hotel to talk to him and ask for things. President Grant called these people "lobbyists" — a term still used today.

Dueling Mr. Decatur

When war hero Stephen Decatur and his wife, Susan, moved to Washington in 1813, they built a house close to the White House on Lafayette Square. Decatur had earned tremendous popularity as a young naval captain in the War of 1812. At the time, Washington insiders agreed he could succeed at politics and perhaps even become president!

But one man stood in the way of Decatur's future. In 1807, Stephen Decatur had served on the trial of Naval Commander James Barron. Barron was brought trial for allowing British officers to board his ship. When Barron went to trial, Decatur was given command of his ship.

Needless to say, Commander Barron wasn't too

PARANORMAL POP QUIZ!

During the War of 1812, British soldiers invaded Washington and set the White House on fire. More than one hundred years later, visitors who have slept at the Executive Mansion have reported seeing an old-fashioned British soldier try to set fire to their bed.
True or false?

(Answer: True)

36

fond of Decatur. Over the years, tensions between the two men grew. Finally, in 1820, Barron challenged Decatur to a duel. In the early morning hours of March 22, 1820, Stephen Decatur left his home without telling his wife where he was going. He met James Barron,

THE PHANTOM FILES

A duel is a formal fight between two people armed with deadly weapons. In the 1800s, people would duel to the death to defend personal honor. Good thing times have changed!

and the men agreed on the terms of the duel: They would walk ten paces, then fire their pistols!

Both men were hit. Though Barron lived, Stephen Decatur died that night at his Lafayette Square home. Washington society was shocked and outraged by Stephen Decatur's death. But some say he never really left this world. . . .

At the Decatur House, which is now a museum, some have sworn they've seen the ghostly war hero peering from a second-story window. Others claim they've spotted the specter of Decatur slipping out the back door of his home — just as he did on the day of his death.

The Haunted Octagon

The stately Washington, D.C., building known as the Octagon was built between 1799 and 1801 for Colonel John Tayloe III, his wife, Anne, and their fifteen children. The house was the site of tragic events that had haunting consequences!

A Spooked Staircase

The Octagon is filled with extraordinary architectural features, including a magnificent spiral staircase. The winding staircase once witnessed a terrible tragedy — and is said to be the *centerpiece* of the house's ghostly activity.

It all began one night almost two hundred years ago. One of Colonel Tayloe's daughters had fallen in love with someone he disapproved of, and father and daughter had a heated argument at the foot of the stairs. According to legend, the daughter angrily stomped up the stairs.

As the colonel was gathering his thoughts and

THE PHANTOM FILES

By definition, an octagon is a structure with eight sides. But the unique Washington house known as the Octagon only has six sides! Now a museum, the house has several round rooms in the front, creating eight angles, which gives the structure its name.

calming down, there was a loud scream and sickening *thud*. The colonel's daughter had somehow fallen and hit the floor! Did she jump to her death, or lose her balance on the stairs' low railing? Her death still remains a mystery. . . .

Tragedy Strikes Again

Tragedy on the Octagon's staircase didn't end there. Another of the

PARANORMAL POP QUIZ!

President James Madison and First Lady Dolley Madison lived in the Octagon while the White House was being rebuilt after a fire during the War of 1812. True or false?

(Answer: *True*)

colonel's daughters fell in love with someone the colonel considered a political enemy. This time, it was a young British officer who was taking part in occupying Washington, D.C., right before the War of 1812. After arguing with her father, Colonel Tayloe's daughter eloped with the young man. Several months later, she returned to the Octagon and encountered her father on the stairs. According to the story, he brushed past her without speaking. She was on the railing side of the staircase, lost her balance, and tumbled down, breaking her neck.

Some say that the colonel's grief over his daughters led to his own untimely death at the age of fifty-four. Though they are long gone,

THE PHANTOM FILES

Historical records show that Dolley Madison threw many parties at the Octagon. People still report seeing the spirit of Dolley Madison standing, and even dancing, where she was once a hostess. Some say that you can even smell the fragrance of lilacs, the former First Lady's favorite perfume!

it's said that both of the colonel's daughters who perished on the infamous staircase still live on at the Octagon.

Supernatural Shadows and Screams

PARANORMAL POP QUIZ!

Some paranormal investigators believe that spirits appear as tiny points of light called lighties. True or false?

(Answer: False. They are called glowies.)

On certain dark nights, some people swear you can see the light of a candle going up the Octagon's staircase, casting a shadow on the opposite wall! And, they say, you can hear bloodcurdling screams and a loud, terrible noise — perhaps the sound of the young women who fell to their deaths in the Octagon. . . .

The colonel's second daughter who died may continue to show her presence in the house — in a most unusual way! When she fell, she landed on the carpet at the foot of the stairs and the carpet turned over. Some say that no matter how many times you turn that carpet over at the Octagon stairs, its edge will always curl back up again, an enduring sign of the girl's tragic end!

Is that curled carpet at the Octagon a true sign of the supernatural? Does the ghost of Lincoln really patrol the White House at midnight? Who knows? But no matter what, now you'll be prepared for a face-to-face encounter with history the next time you're in our nation's capital!

THE PHANTOM FILES

The Library of Congress in Washington, D.C., is said to house a helpful ghost: a police officer who lives in the stacks! He may appear both in uniform and in plainclothes — either way, the kind ghost aids people who are lost in the vast array of bookshelves by directing them to exits!

This is a view of Independence Hall in Philadelphia, Pennsylvania. Legend has it that the ghosts of America's Founding Fathers — among a few other spirits — haunt this historic landmark.

Bettmann/Corbis

THE HISTORY CHANNEL

This painting shows Betsy Ross sewing America's first flag. Many claim that Ross's polite phantom still lingers in her Philadelphia home.

A SCRIBNER STORYBOOK
Classic

TREASURE
+ ISLAND +

ROBERT LOUIS STEVENSON
illustrated by N. C. WYETH

THE HISTORY CHANNEL

The book *Treasure Island*, by Robert Louis Stevenson, is an exciting adventure about pirates. According to local Savannah legend, one of the characters in the book was based on a real-life pirate who visited the former inn (and modern-day restaurant) Pirates' House . . . and whose ghost may remain there!

The lush, mysterious Bonaventure Cemetery in Savannah, Georgia, is rumored to be haunted by the ghosts of Colonel Tattnall and his party guests, who still think they're at a long-ago celebration....

THE HISTORY CHANNEL®

This is a nighttime view of the White House, located in Washington, D.C. It's said that late at night, spirits of long-dead Presidents and First Ladies wander the halls of this stately building.

THE HISTORY CHANNEL®

Welcome to two of Chicago's most famously spooky cemeteries! The entryway to St. James the Sag (top) doesn't hint at the ghosts that are rumored to reside there. But a crooked gate at Bachelor's Grove (bottom) certainly seems creepy. . . .

This is legendary attorney Clarence Darrow. Many have claimed to see a ghostly figure walking the Chicago streets wearing a hat and trench coat . . . and some believe it's the spirit of the long-gone lawyer!

Here, visitors study the front of the Winchester Mystery House in San Jose, California. This strange structure is the legacy of Sarah Winchester, who kept building additions to the house in order to ward off spirits. But many think the house may be haunted by its former owner!

Richard T. Nowitz/Corbis

④ CHICAGO, ILLINOIS

CHILLING CEMETERIES (AND MORE) IN THE WINDY CITY

Called the Windy City for its blustery weather, Chicago is said to be haunted by many spirits from its colorful history. Interested in ghostly monks, mobsters, or mutts? You go, ghoul — and check out Chicago's fascinating cast of phantasms!

CHILLING CEMETERIES

Chicago has not one, but *two*, cemeteries chock-full of restless spirits. Take your pick: Bachelor's Grove Cemetery, said to be the most haunted graveyard in the Midwest, or the cemetery at St. James the Sag, the oldest in Chicago, where ghost sightings have occurred for years. Can't decide? That's okay — let's check out both!

St. James the Sag's Phantom Monks

Founded in 1833 by Irish immigrants, the parish of St. James became known as "the Sag"

THE PHANTOM FILES

The roots of Chicago are found in the place where the Chicago River joins Lake Michigan. Explorers Louis Jolliet and Father Jacques Marquette first spotted the Indian village called Checagou there in 1673. The name meant "that which is strong"!

because it is next to the Sag Bridge (short for Saganashkee Slough), which crosses the Des Plains River. As workers began building the Illinois and Michigan Canal in 1836, the parish grew.

Those who came to Chicago to build the canal endured terrible living conditions, from backbreaking work to poor sanitation and rampant disease. As a result, many of the workers died and were buried at St. James the Sag. It's said that groups of ghostly monks still roam the woods around the cemetery, perhaps continuing to offer spiritual aid to long-gone workers. According to Richard Crowe, St. James the Sag's monks appear in groups of three. "I have police reports from people who've actually seen and encountered these people at night," says Crowe.

A Forbidden Romance

The monks aren't the only religious figures in

residence at the church. It's said that a young priest from the distant past is often seen at St. James the Sag, remaining there with the love of his life.

When a young priest at the church fell in love with a parishioner, the couple decided to elope. They planned to secretly meet on a hill beside the church one moonlit night, then drive away in a horse-drawn buggy.

The young couple met as planned. But as they rode away, a terrible accident killed both the priest and his beloved. Although they were not allowed to be buried at the church cemetery, it's said that they are still there every day.

As far back as the 1890s, people have reported seeing a phantom horse and carriage. There have also been reports of a woman dressed in white —

THE PHANTOM FILES

Rumor has it that the gravesites at St. James the Sag heave up and down, as if something beneath the earth is *breathing*. . . .

who dances in the church roadway! Could these be traces of the long-lost couple?

Bachelor's Grove Cemetery: Spirits Galore!

Bachelor's Grove Cemetery is located deep in the forest in Chicago's southern suburbs. There, it's said, the ghost of a murderous cemetery caretaker appears next to a phantom farmhouse. And there are many other strange events at the cemetery, say witnesses.

When vandals dug up graves at Bachelor's Grove Cemetery, Melissa Stubblefield and other volunteers worked to repair the

THE PHANTOM FILES

Bachelor's Grove Cemetery dates back to the 1830s, when men traveled from the East without their families — as "bachelors" — to settle homesteads on the prairie. After they had established their farms, their families would follow.

damage — and had a few encounters with not-so-friendly resident spirits! "There were apples being thrown at us. . . . I know that they were there and I could sense they were very, very mad," says Ms. Stubblefield. But once the volunteers filled in the graves, the spirits started to calm down. "There wasn't as much a sense of them being mad anymore," she says. Ms. Stubblefield is one of many people who claim to have seen odd lighted orbs floating through Bachelor's Grove. Witnesses say the orbs — round, glowing balls that float through the air — appear in many different sizes and in colors such as blue, red, orange, and white.

PARANORMAL POP QUIZ!

In the early 1830s, Chicago was a sophisticated, large city that many compared to Boston at the time. True or false?

(Answer: False — Chicago in the 1830s has been described as "not much more than a fur-trading post.")

The Women of Bachelor's Grove

Two white-clad female figures are said to be among the spirits who dwell at the old cemetery. The first, known as the Madonna of Bachelor's Grove, is frequently spied wandering the gravesite grounds. The ghostly apparition walks slowly through the cemetery, carrying a tiny infant.

A grislier tale is told about another woman in white at Bachelor's Grove. It's said that long ago, a man killed his girlfriend, and she was buried in the cemetery. Though she is long gone, she's not forgotten. . . . According to local legend, the young woman vowed to avenge her terrible death — and spends her afterlife stalking young men. Some say the ghostly being draws young men to Bachelor's Grove—and chops their heads off!

THE LAWYER WHO WON'T LEAVE?

Chicago's magnificent Museum of Science and Industry was originally built for the World's Fair of 1893 — and today, it is one of the city's greatest treasures. The museum still has amazing exhibits . . . and its grounds are said to be haunted by the ghost of a world-famous lawyer.

Chicago's Clarence Darrow was one of the greatest lawyers of all time and was often called "attorney for the damned" because he would accept cases that no one else would touch! Darrow frequently represented poor clients. He built a reputation as a brilliant legal mind through the 1920s and 1930s.

When Darrow died in March 1938, his ashes

PARANORMAL POP QUIZ!
Chicago has made it through good times and bad with the city motto: "I can." True or false?

(Answer: False. The city motto is "I will.")

48

were scattered in Jackson Park, not far from his Chicago home. The park, which is behind the Museum of Science and Industry, features a bridge dedicated to Darrow's memory. Since Darrow's death, many have claimed that *more* than his ashes remain at the park.

A number of people have reported seeing a ghostly figure standing on the bridge or walking behind the museum. The man wears a 1930s-style trench coat and fedora, say witnesses.

Folklorist Richard Crowe made one such sighting in 1995 — on Halloween! Mr. Crowe says, "[The figure] was dressed in the fashion of the 1930s, [wearing something that] someone of prominence, someone of importance would wear.

THE PHANTOM FILES

Clarence Darrow represented Nathan Leopold and Richard Loeb, college students found guilty of kidnapping and murdering fourteen-year-old Bobby Franks. Leopold and Loeb were both sent to prison. Some say Bobby Franks's spirit appeared at his gravesite throughout the years that Leopold and Loeb lived. By 1971, they had both died — and Bobby's ghost disappeared!

He walked down the sidewalk and stopped directly in front of the rear doors of the museum. He stared down the water's edge, stayed there for a while, and then he turned and walked back the way he came."

And what did coming face-to-face with a spirit — one of the world's greatest attorneys, no less — feel like? "It was one of the most unique experiences of my life," says Mr. Crowe. "I'm sure that figure that I saw that night had to be the ghost of Clarence Darrow."

GHOSTS IN GANGLAND

The 2002 hit movie *Chicago* showed the criminal side of the city during the roaring 1920s. In real life, legendary battles between Chicago's criminal gangs resulted in a string of mobster murders at the time. Gang leader Al Capone decided to end it all on February 14, 1929.

Capone had his men dress up as Chicago police officers and conduct a fake "raid" on rival George "Bugs" Moran's headquarters at the SMC Cartage Company. Moran's men believed the "police" were real, lined up against the wall, and were executed with machine guns!

That grisly event shocked the world — and became known as the St. Valentine's Day Massacre. It's said that the dreadful killings sparked a series of hauntings and other strange events that continue to this day.

THE PHANTOM FILES

Many believe that the murky waters of Bachelor's Grove Cemetery may contain the bodies of the victims from Chicago's gang wars of the 1920s. Some say the ghosts of those dumped there still haunt the place!

Gangster Ghosts

Although the SMC Cartage Company was torn down in 1967, many say the ghosts of gangsters remain there. But according to author Ursula Bielski, witnesses to the ghostly men say they seem more confused than dangerous. "[Witnesses will] see shadowy figures seemingly all dressed up, kind of with no place to go, wandering around aimlessly," she reports.

Canine Sixth Sense?

Though most remember that seven people died in the St. Valentine's Day Massacre, many do not know that a German shepherd named Highball was at the crime scene that day. Highball was the pet of John May, an auto mechanic for the Moran gang — and one of the men killed. While his owner was shot, Highball was tied to a car bumper.

PARANORMAL POP QUIZ!

Animals are believed to have a sixth sense for ghosts that is as strong, if not stronger, than that of humans. True or false?

(Answer: True)

Highball's mournful wails brought neighbors to the grisly scene. The poor dog could not be calmed. In fact, he was so upset, he had to be put to sleep!

More than seventy years later, people still notice that their pets begin to act up and become agitated when they walk past the crime scene. Do dogs today have a sixth sense about poor Highball? Or is it simply a coincidence?

Bad Luck Bricks

Perhaps it's also a coincidence that the bricks from the building where men were murdered seem to bring bad luck. Or perhaps, some say, the building's bricks are truly cursed.

A man who had taken four bricks as souvenirs from the St. Valentine's Day Massacre site had terrible luck — and all the bad things happened in fours! He went through four divorces, had quadruple bypass heart surgery, and had a kidney removed because of four polyps (a polyp is a growth on an organ that can be harmful).

Other souvenir hunters swear they never would have taken the bricks if they had known the trouble it would bring to their lives. In fact, Chicago brick collector Jan Gabriel believes the bricks were the cause of his failed marriages and health problems. Gabriel has had his "pieces of history" for some time . . . but now intends to destroy them!

THE COUNTRY HOUSE HAUNTINGS

The Country House restaurant in Clarendon Hills, one of Chicago's suburbs, was built in the 1920s. Today, the restaurant still hosts some very special guests — who visited a long time ago and never left!

Floating Phantom

When handyman Frank Wadzulis was fixing the Country House's rest rooms one night, he heard music coming from the restaurant's juke-box. Strangely, the same song kept play-ing over and over. Even stranger, Frank was alone — and had turned off the power in the restaurant!

Frank was shocked to see a woman *stand-ing* at the jukebox. But when he looked closer,

THE PHANTOM FILES

In the 1990s, psychologist James Houran used a video camera and a special microphone to investigate ghostly activity at the Country House. The microphone picked up odd sounds in "hot spots," and the camera found "bursts" of electromagnetic radiation. Some believe such energy is a sure sign of ghosts....

he saw that she wasn't really standing! "There was nothing from the bottom of the dress to the floor — no legs, no feet...nothing," he recalls.

Behind the Music

Did the mysterious woman standing at the jukebox really exist? Some say yes. Author

Ursula Bielski says that in the 1950s, a woman and her child came into the restaurant one day. The woman asked the staff if she could leave her child there for a while. The staff refused, and the lady left. According to Bielski, "She was flustered, disappointed, seemed confused as she left the bar. They found not long after that she had driven her car into a tree not a mile down the road." Many think the mysterious figure by the jukebox is the spirit of this woman.

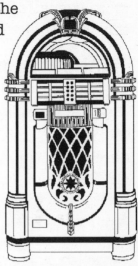

Plates that Fly?

Country House assistant manager Eileen Grogan was in the kitchen one evening when she heard the crash of a plate falling on the floor. That wasn't so strange. But she wasn't prepared for what happened next. . . .

"I looked and saw a

PARANORMAL POP QUIZ!

Try as they might, ghost hunters are unable to record spirit sounds of any kind. True or false?

(Answer: False. Some ghost hunters have recorded a variety of eerie sounds!)

55

plate actually come off the pile of plates and go across horizontally and land on the floor. About two or three plates actually crashed in front of me. They didn't fall off the stack; they actually levitated across the kitchen and fell to the floor," says Grogan.

THE PHANTOM FILES

A spiritual medium called in to investigate strange events at the Country House "sensed" an incident involving a woman, a child, and an accident in the 1950s!

What caused the plates to fly at the Country House? Eileen has no idea. But, she says, "I don't think it was anything that I can explain."

Chicago's varied and exciting past has produced some amazing tales of hauntings. And as long as Lake Michigan's waves cascade along the Chicago waterfront, these spooky tales will be told. And there may be more

PARANORMAL POP QUIZ!

The noisy, mischievous ghosts known as poltergeists are often blamed for breaking things. True or false?

(Answer: True)

ghostly happenings waiting to take place. Who knows what will "blow in" on your next visit to the Windy City?

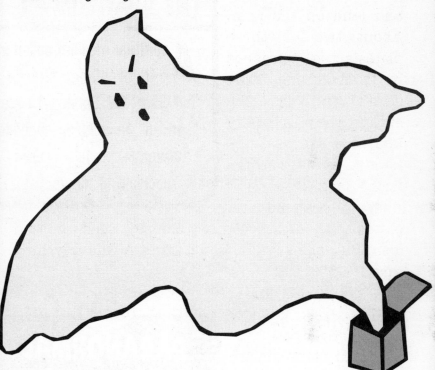

5

SAN FRANCISCO, CALIFORNIA

CREEPY MANSIONS AND GOLD RUSH GHOSTS

During the California gold rush, from 1848 to 1850, San Francisco grew from a sleepy town of less than nine hundred people to a boomtown of 56,000! Some believe that San Francisco's rough-and-tumble past left the city with some of the scariest — and strangest — ghosts in the West!

WINCHESTER MYSTERY HOUSE

With its magnificent turrets, towers, and stained-glass windows, the Winchester House is a grand structure and a California Historical

Landmark. The 160-room mansion (now known as the Winchester Mystery House) is open to the public and, once the site of regular seances, it may still be home to ghosts. . . .

The Medium and Mrs. Winchester

Growing up in Connecticut, Sarah Pardee was a popular and well-educated young woman known as "the Belle of New Haven." In 1862, she married a man named William Winchester, whose family business had created the Winchester repeating rifle. Used with deadly results in the Civil War and on the American frontier, the weapon earned a reputation as "the Gun That Won the West," creating a vast fortune for the Winchester family.

THE PHANTOM FILES

The island of Alcatraz — sometimes called Devil's Island — in San Francisco Bay became a harsh maximum-security prison in 1934. Now a museum, Alcatraz may still be home to criminal spirits. Rangers there have reported unexplained screams, crashes — and cell doors that close by themselves!

Not long after Sarah's marriage to William Winchester, tragedy struck. In 1866, their infant daughter died. Soon after, William Winchester died while still in his forties. Sarah inherited twenty million dollars from her husband's rifle business, but came to believe that her terrible misfortune was also linked to the deadly legacy of the Winchester rifle.

It's said that a medium in Boston told Sarah that the angry spirits of people killed by the Winchester repeating rifle caused the deaths of her child and husband. There was just one way Sarah could calm those spirits, said the medium. She must keep on building a house and never finish it!

Séances in San Jose

In 1884, Sarah left Connecticut for California and bought a small farmhouse in San Jose, about fifty miles outside of San Francisco. She took the advice of her spiritualist and began building on to the farmhouse to ward off the Winchester curse.

PARANORMAL POP QUIZ!

To reach San Francisco during the gold rush years, fortune hunters first had to survive a long and risky journey around the tip of South America by boat or across the American prairie by covered wagon. True or false?

(Answer: True. The transcontinental railroad wasn't finished until 1869, so cross-country trains were not yet available!)

For thirty-eight years, Sarah had teams of carpenters working on the house around the clock, through weekends and holidays! Precisely at midnight and again at two A.M. each evening, a bell would toll from the ever-growing house. Many believe that during those hours, Sarah Winchester retired to a special séance room to contact

THE PHANTOM FILES

Sarah Winchester was fascinated with the number thirteen. Many of her house's stairways have thirteen steps. Thirteen palm trees line the driveway, and all the ceiling and wall panels are made in thirteen sections. The house has thirteen bathrooms — and the thirteenth bathroom has thirteen windows. The kitchen sink has thirteen drain holes, and the house has a special chandelier with thirteen lights!

THE PHANTOM FILES

A person who is said to be able to contact and even attract spirits is called a medium. During a séance, a medium might go into a trance, and the spirit is said to speak "through" that person. Pretty creepy, huh?

spirits from the netherworld. It's said that her spirit advisers gave her the plans for the next room to build.

Sarah would draw

her ideas of designs for the house. Based on Winchester's sketches, the house is like no other in the world. It has staircases that lead to ceilings, doors that open into solid walls, and other doors that lead nowhere at all! Some say Sarah's strange designs were meant to confuse the spirits that she believed pursued her.

Spirits Still at Work?

THE PHANTOM FILES

Many ghosts inhabit places because they're still waiting for something to happen there, says psychic Annette Martin. "They're people waiting for a command or instructions," she explains. Perhaps spirits hang around the Winchester Mystery House because they want someone to say that construction is finally done. . . .

SPOOKY

When Sarah Winchester died in 1922, construction on the house came to a stop. But witnesses say that some *spirits* are still hard at work on the house!

In fact, Winchester Mystery House restoration expert Jack Stubbert says he and a coworker came face-to-face with another worker . . . from the past. An eerie, translucent figure came into the hallway, stood in front of the stairway, then turned and looked right at them!

The figure then walked up the stairs. According to Stubbert, "I figured somebody was in the house, except, you know, it was that transparent look. It gives you a funny feeling."

The Spirit of Sarah

Some witnesses say that Sarah Winchester's *own* spirit is in residence at the mansion. During all the years of construction, Sarah Winchester had little contact with the outside world and never allowed her picture to be taken. However, in recent years, she's presented herself to visitors in extraordinary ways.

According to Winchester Mystery House employee Shozo Kagoshima, many visitors report seeing a red ball of light in the room where Sarah died. The orb travels across the room toward the bed —

PARANORMAL POP QUIZ!

When the San Francisco earthquake of 1906 wrecked a seven-story tower and other portions of the Winchester House, Sarah ordered that thirty rooms in the house be closed up — forever! True or false?

(Answer: True)

then disappears! Even odder, some claim to have actually seen Sarah, looking as she did in the past. According to Kagoshima, an employee who was going through the house for the first time swears she spotted the ghostly, silent figure. "She saw a woman dressed in Victorian clothing sitting at one of the kitchen tables," Kagoshima says.

THE HAUNTED SPEAKEASY

San Francisco is home to spirits from more modern times as well. During the Prohibition years in the 1920s, selling alcoholic beverages was against the law. Secret speakeasies — places that continued to sell liquor — sprang up throughout the city. On the isolated coast of Half Moon Bay, just south of San Francisco, a former speakeasy is said to be haunted.

Bootlegger Bay

In 1920, a quiet stretch of Half Moon Bay known as Moss Beach became the place where secret — or "boot-legged" — alcohol would reach San Francisco. Ships from Canada would anchor out about three miles from the coastline, then fishing boats would race out to unload the illegal cargo and bring it back to shore! Perched high above the dangerous action was a speakeasy called Frank's Place. The speakeasy attracted a lively crowd, including a woman known only as the Blue Lady. Though long gone, many say that she still makes her presence known at Moss Beach.

THE PHANTOM FILES

The ghost of murdered U.S. Senator David Broderick is said to haunt an 1851 house that overlooks San Francisco Bay. Senator Broderick opposed slavery; his killer supported it. Senator Broderick died before slavery was abolished, and many believe the loud footsteps and odd tapping in the house are the senator, returning to continue his fight against slavery....

Deadly Jealousy

It's said that an unhappily married woman who always dressed in blue often visited Frank's Place in the 1920s. One night, her husband found her talking with the piano player at the roadhouse. Later, her body was found on the beach below.

Did the woman's jealous husband stab her to death? Nobody knows for sure. But the Blue Lady is said to haunt the sites of her sad life and brutal murder.

PARANORMAL POP QUIZ!

A recent poll found that close to one-third of Americans believe in ghosts — and fourteen percent have reported experiencing one! True or false?

(Answer: True)

The ghostly figure of the Blue Lady has been seen hovering above the waves on Moss Beach. But more often, witnesses say her spirit lurks in the old speakeasy, which is no longer called Frank's Place. It is now an elegant restaurant named the Moss Beach Distillery — but it's still said to be the site of otherworldly occurrences!

Swinging from Chandeliers?

At the Moss Beach Distillery, some say there are sounds of laughter, glasses clinking, and footsteps coming from empty rooms. Others claim that shadows appear in the stairwell — when nobody is there.

But few incidents at the restaurant are

stranger than the experience of former manager Ellen King. She witnessed *something* — or a ghostly someone — that seemed to swing from a large lamp in the restaurant!

The huge, heavy glass lamp that sits over the hostess stand at the front of the restaurant never budges, not even in windy weather. But one evening, says King, "I glanced [over] and I [saw] the lamp moving. And [it wasn't] moving half an inch, [it was] moving significantly." King and a coworker checked windows and doors and saw that none were open. So it wasn't wind that caused the wild swinging.

Was it a supernatural presence, such as the Blue Lady, that was actually *swinging*

THE PHANTOM FILES

Employees at the Moss Beach Distillery have reported seeing a huge, misty ball of something resembling smoke appear under the restaurant's large glass lamp. Some paranormal experts say that certain ghosts appear as misty or hazy spheres!

from the lamp? It's hard to say for sure, but many believe that the Blue Lady is behind such peculiar incidents.

THE MANSIONS

In 1887, millionaire Richard Craig Chambers built a grand house in the middle of San Francisco. Later, the private home became a fancy hotel called the Mansions. It's said that the rambling house is filled to the rafters with spirits!

A Bizarre Accident

When Chambers died in 1901, he left his mansion to his niece Claudia and her sister. Claudia was said to be an eccentric character who met a strange end on the mansion's third floor.

Some say that Claudia was stabbed to death. Others claim she was actually sawed in half! In any case, the young woman's uneasy soul is said to still hover around the hotel today. The creepy feeling that many experience when they enter the room on the third floor where Claudia died is just the beginning. . . .

PARANORMAL POP QUIZ!

According to paranormal investigators, ghosts never appear during the day. True or false?

(Answer: False. Though more often spotted at night, some ghosts do appear during daylight hours.)

68

Ghosts in the Bathroom?

Mansions Hotel employee Bismark Valle recently had a bizarre experience in one of the hotel's rooms. He recalls that when he was alone, checking the room, the television turned on by itself — and the toilet began to flush, again and again! When he turned the television off, it inexplicably turned itself on again.

THE PHANTOM FILES

Experts say that some ghosts appear as shadows. They may be up to ten feet tall and are sometimes seen darting through walls!

"It's not a remote-control TV," reports Valle, certain that the incident wasn't a mechanical mishap. "I was scared because it [had] never happened to me [before]. I didn't believe in ghosts. But now I do," he says.

Blasting Books

A peculiar incident in the hotel's presidential suite may be a sign of the supernatural. According to Mansions Hotel owner Bob Pritikin, the suite contains about two thousand books. A woman staying in the suite reported that one morning, one of the books seemed to blast off the bookshelf!

Says Pritikin, "One of the books literally blew out of the bookshelf and across the room and smashed her cosmetic case. And we have that book." The book's title? *The Wind Bloweth*!

Psychic Proof

With so many reports of strange sightings and curious incidents, Bob Pritikin decided to invite a team of psychic researchers to investigate. The most logical place to start? The room that once belonged to the mysterious Claudia, of course!

As they conducted the séance, a potted palm in the room began to move as if there were a strong wind in the room — but there was no wind at all! Soon after, a wineglass on a table suddenly exploded into hundreds of tiny pieces — when no one had touched it.

Sensing that they were absolutely not alone, the team sent down for a camera, reports Pritikin. "They had the front desk person rushed up at their request and snap a picture," he says. And what did it record? "We actually have a photograph of the ghost floating in that room," claims Pritikin.

70

For sheer weirdness, San Francisco's alleged specters are in a league of their own. But then, the ghostly graveyards and spooky spots across America each have their own special, chilling stories that makes them unique. Perhaps there are even some incredible ghostly tales floating around in your *own* hometown!

GHOSTLY GRAVEYARDS AND SPOOKY SPOTS: THE ULTIMATE CHALLENGE

Congratulations, spirit seekers! You've successfully explored some of America's most haunted sites! But how much do you remember about the spirits you've encountered? Test your ghostly knowledge . . . if you dare!

1. **Sarah Winchester's home shows her fascination with:**
   a. spiders
   b. the number thirteen
   c. weapons

2. **Benjamin Franklin was a writer, a publisher, and:**
   a. a doctor
   b. a farmer
   c. an inventor

3. **Chicago's Clarence Darrow was known for being:**
   a. a great attorney
   b. a great physician
   c. a great politician

4. **Which famous author is linked to ghostly activity in Philadelphia?**
   a. Edgar Allan Poe
   b. Mary Shelley
   c. Jack London

5. **Savannah's Bonaventure Cemetery is said to be the site of:**
   a. a never-ending party
   b. a never-ending battle
   c. a never-ending family feud

72

6. **This ghostly First Lady is one of Washington, D.C.'s most-seen specters:**
   a. Martha Washington
   b. Dolley Madison
   c. Mamie Eisenhower

7. **The island where the former federal penitentiary of Alcatraz is located is sometimes called:**
   a. Criminal Island
   b. Swimming Seal Island
   c. Devil's Island

8. **The name of the dog who was a witness to the St. Valentine's Day massacre was:**
   a. Cocktail
   b. Lowball
   c. Highball

9. **Before the tragic deaths of his two daughters, how many children did Colonel John Tayloe have?**
   a. seven
   b. fifteen
   c. twelve

10. **The Pirates' House in Savannah is supposedly the real-life setting for a famous scene in the novel:**
    a. *Treasure Island*
    b. *The Swiss Family Robinson*
    c. *Mutiny on the Bounty*

Answers: 1. b, 2. c, 3. a, 4. a, 5. c, 6. b, 7. c, 8. c, 9. b, 10. a.

73

GHOSTLY GLOSSARY

ANESTHETIC: (ahn-ih-stet-ik) a drug that numbs feeling or pain.

APPARITION: (a-puh-RIH-shun) the appearance or vision of a person; a ghost.

BUCCANEER: (buck-ah-near) a pirate.

CLAIRVOYANCE: (klar-VOY-ants) the ability to gather information paranormally. A clairvoyant is a person who may be able to sense and explain ghost activity.

DIGNITARY: (dig-NAH-tair-ee) a person holding a high position or office.

LOBBYIST: (lob-ee-ist) a person who tries to get politicians to support or vote for a specific cause or issue.

MEDIUM: (mee-dee-um) a person through whom spirits speak or act.

PARANORMAL: (pa-ruh-NOR-muhl) beyond the normal; something that cannot be explained scientifically or through ordinary knowledge.

PHANTASM: (FAN-ta-zuhm) a ghost or an apparition.

POLTERGEIST: (POHL-ter-gyst) a noisy or troublesome spirit. A poltergeist might be responsible for unexplained movement of objects, noises, and physically bothering a person.

SPECTER: (SPEHK-ter) a ghost or an apparition.